**REALLY EASY GUITAR**

# ALTERNATIVE ROCK

## 22 SONGS WITH CHORDS, LYRICS & BASIC TAB

ISBN 978-1-70516-557-7

Visit Hal Leonard Online at
**www.halleonard.com**

World headquarters, contact:
**Hal Leonard**
7777 West Bluemound Road
Milwaukee, WI 53213
Email: info@halleonard.com

In Europe, contact:
**Hal Leonard Europe Limited**
1 Red Place
London, W1K 6PL
Email: info@halleonardeurope.com

In Australia, contact:
**Hal Leonard Australia Pty. Ltd.**
4 Lentara Court
Cheltenham, Victoria, 3192 Australia
Email: info@halleonard.com.au

# GUITAR NOTATION LEGEND

## Chord Diagrams

**CHORD DIAGRAMS** graphically represent the guitar fretboard to show correct chord fingerings.
- The letter above the diagram tells the name of the chord.
- The top, bold horizontal line represents the nut of the guitar. Each thin horizontal line represents a fret. Each vertical line represents a string; the low E string is on the far left and the high E string is on the far right.
- A dot shows where to put your fret-hand finger and the number at the bottom of the diagram tells which finger to use.
- The "O" above the string means play it open, while an "X" means don't play the string.

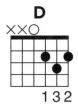

## Tablature

**TABLATURE** graphically represents the guitar fingerboard. Each horizontal line represents a string, and each number represents a fret.

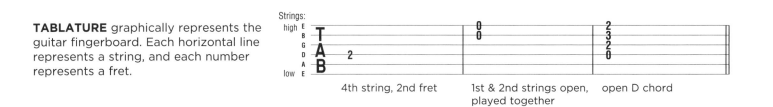

4th string, 2nd fret | 1st & 2nd strings open, played together | open D chord

## Definitions for Special Guitar Notation

**HAMMER-ON:** Strike the first (lower) note with one finger, then sound the higher note (on the same string) with another finger by fretting it without picking.

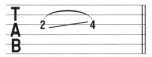

**PULL-OFF:** Place both fingers on the notes to be sounded. Strike the first note and without picking, pull the finger off to sound the second (lower) note.

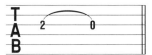

**LEGATO SLIDE:** Strike the first note and then slide the same fret-hand finger up or down to the second note. The second note is not struck.

**SHIFT SLIDE:** Same as legato slide, except the second note is struck.

## Additional Musical Definitions

**N.C.**  • No chord. Instrument is silent.

• Repeat measures between signs.

# Alive

Words by Eddie Vedder
Music by Stone Gossard

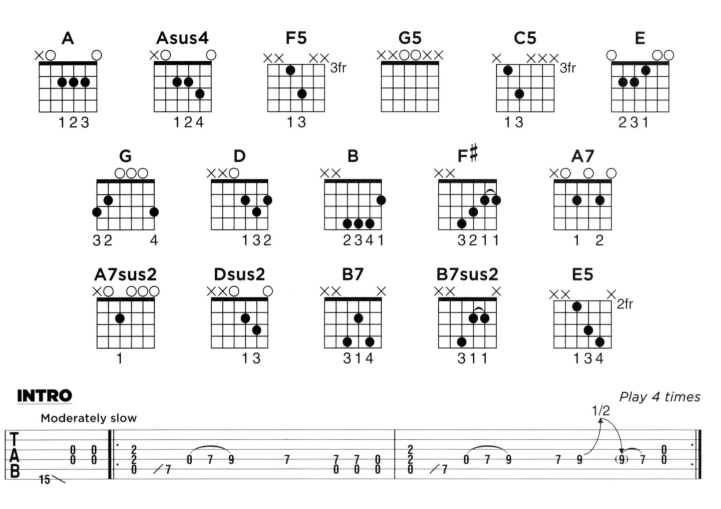

## INTRO

Moderately slow

*Play 4 times*

## VERSE 1

A   Asus4    A     Asus4
"Son,"     she said,   "Have I got a little story for you.

A   Asus4          A   Asus4
What you thought was your daddy    was nothing but a...

A   Asus4         A    Asus4
While you were sitting home alone at age thirteen,

A   Asus4         A   Asus4
your real daddy was dying.

             F5    G5 C5     F5     G5 C5
Sorry you didn't see him.     But I'm glad we talked."

## CHORUS 1

```
      E    G   D       A
Oh, I'm,  oh,  I'm still alive.

      E    G   D       A
Aay, I'm,  oh,  I'm still alive.

      E    G   D       A         B
Aay, I'm,  oh,  I'm still alive, aay, oh,    oh.
```

## VERSE 2

```
 A  Asus4              A   Asus4
 While she walks slowly    across a young man's room,

 A  Asus4              A   Asus4
   she said, "I'm ready        for you."

 A  Asus4          A        Asus4
 I can't remember anything to this very day,

 A  Asus4          A      Asus4
  'cept the love,    the love.

    F5              G5  C5     F5     G5  C5
Oh, you know where,      now I    can see.
```

## CHORUS 2

```
      E    G  D        A
I just stare,  I,  I'm still alive.

      E    G   D       A
Aay, I'm,  oh,  I'm still alive.

      E    G   D       A
Aay, I'm,  oh,  I'm still alive.

      E    G   D       A
Aay, I'm,  oh,  I'm still alive, aay.
```

## BRIDGE

*Play 3 times*

```
| B              | F#          | : B            | F#          :|
```

```
A7  A7sus2  Dsus2              A7     A7sus2  Dsus2
    "Is something wrong?" she said.

    A7   A7sus2  Dsus2              A7      A7sus2  Dsus2
Of course there is.       "You're still alive," she said.

        B7  B7sus2  E5              B7   B7sus2  E5
Oh, and do I deserve to be?       Is that the question?

        B7  B7sus2  E5       B7   B7sus2  E5
And if so,    if     so, who answers?    Who answers?
```

## CHORUS 3

**E   G   D      A**
I'm,   oh,  I'm still alive.

**E   G   D      A**
Aay, I'm,  oh,  I'm still alive.

**E   G   D      A**
Aay, I'm,  oh,  I'm still alive.

**E   G       D  A**
Aay, I'm,  oo,  I'm still alive,     yeah, yeah, yeah, yeah, yeah, yeah.

## GUITAR SOLO

*Play 9 times*

‖: E     G    | D    A    | E    G    | D    A    :‖ E        |

‖

# Black Hole Sun

### Words and Music by Chris Cornell

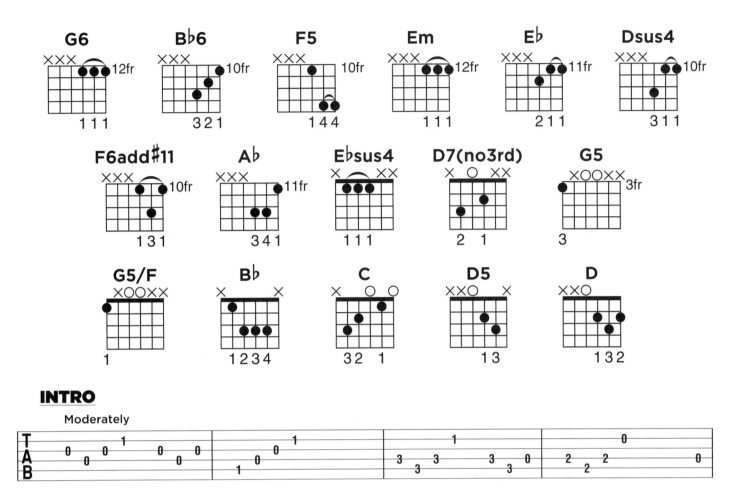

## INTRO

Moderately

## VERSE 1

**G6**      **Bb6**     **F5**         **Em**
In my eyes, indisposed, in disguise as no one knows,

    **Eb**    **Dsus4**     **G6**    **F6add#11** **Ab**
hides the face, lies the snake, the sun in my disgrace.

**G6**      **Bb6**        **F5**           **Em**
Boiling heat, summer stench, 'neath the black, the sky looks dead.

    **Eb**       **Dsus4**    **G6**    **F6add#11** **Ab**
Call my name through the cream, and I'll hear you scream again.

## CHORUS 1

        E♭sus4         D7(no3rd) G5      G5/F     B♭
Black hole sun, won't you come     and wash away the rain?

        E♭sus4         D7(no3rd)       C             D5
Black hole sun, won't you come? Won't you come? Won't you come?


## VERSE 2

      G6         B♭6        F5          Em
Stuttering, cold and damp, steal the warm wind, tired friend,

         E♭     Dsus4         G6    F6add♯11  A♭
times are gone for honest men, and sometimes far too long for  snakes.

      G6         B♭6        F5          Em
In my shoes, a walking sleep, and my youth I pray to keep.

         E♭     Dsus4    G6      F6add♯11  A♭
Heaven send hell away, no one sings like you   anymore.


## CHORUS 2

        E♭sus4         D7(no3rd) G5      G5/F     B♭
Black hole sun, won't you come     and wash away the rain?

        E♭sus4         D7(no3rd)     C    B♭
Black hole sun, won't you come? Won't you come?

        E♭sus4         D7(no3rd) G5      G5/F     B♭
Black hole sun, won't you come     and wash away the rain?

        E♭sus4         D7(no3rd)
Black hole sun, won't you come? Won't you come?


## BRIDGE

   C        B♭         D
   Black hole sun, black hole sun. Won't you come?

   C        B♭         D
   Black hole sun, black hole sun. Won't you come?

   C        B♭         D
   Black hole sun, black hole sun. Won't you come?

   C        B♭         D
   Black hole sun, black hole sun. Won't you come?


## GUITAR SOLO

*Play 6 times*

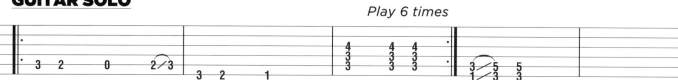

## VERSE 2

                G6            Bb6       F5           Em

Hang my head, drown my fear, 'til you all just disappear.

## CHORUS 3

              Ebsus4           D7(no3rd) G5     G5/F    Bb

Black hole sun, won't you come     and wash away the rain?

              Ebsus4           D7(no3rd)         C     Bb

Black hole sun, won't you come? Won't you come?

              Ebsus4           D7(no3rd) G5     G5/F    Bb

Black hole sun, won't you come     and wash away the rain?

              Ebsus4           D7(no3rd)

Black hole sun, won't you come? Won't you come?

## OUTRO

C         Bb            D

  Black hole sun, black hole sun. Won't you come?

C         Bb            D

  Black hole sun, black hole sun. Won't you come?

C         Bb            D

  Black hole sun, black hole sun. Won't you come?

C         Bb            D

  Black hole sun, black hole sun. Won't you come?

C         Bb            D

  Black hole sun, black hole sun. Won't you come?

C         Bb            D

  Black hole sun, black hole sun. Won't you come?

| C | | Bb | | D | |
|---|---|---|---|---|---|

                                                          Won't you come?

| C | | Bb | | D | |
|---|---|---|---|---|---|

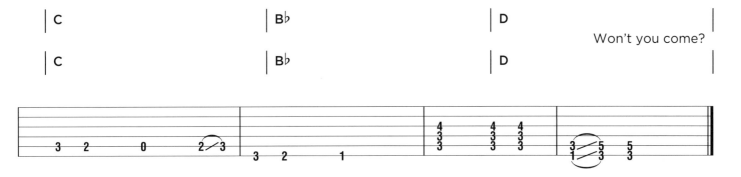

# Drive

Words and Music by Brandon Boyd, Michael Einziger, Alex Katunich,
Jose Pasillas II and Chris Kilmore

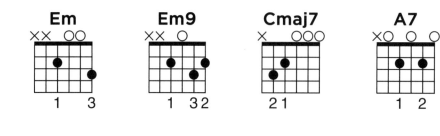

## INTRO

Moderately

‖: Em    Em9 | Cmaj7    A7 |    Em    Em9 | Cmaj7    A7 :‖

## VERSE 1

Em         Em9  Cmaj7         A7
   Sometimes      I feel the fear of

   Em                Em9   Cmaj7  A7
uncertainty stinging clear.

Em      Em9         Cmaj7            A7
   And I,      I can't help but ask myself      how much I'll

Em                Em9       Cmaj7  A7
let the fear take the wheel and steer.

## PRE-CHORUS 1

Cmaj7                    A7              Cmaj7   A7
   It's driven me before, and it seems to have a vague      haunting mass appeal.

Cmaj7        A7              Cmaj7          A7
   But lately I'm beginning to find that I      should be the one behind the wheel.

## CHORUS

Em         Em9 Cmaj7    A7
   Whatever tomor - row brings, I'll be

Em         Em9    Cmaj7         A7
   there with open arms and open eyes, yeah.

Em         Em9 Cmaj7         A7
   Whatever tomor - row brings, I'll be

Em      Em9  Cmaj7      A7
   there, I'll be        there.

## VERSE 2

```
Em        Em9   Cmaj7             A7
     So if I      decide to waver my      chance to

Em               Em9   Cmaj7   A7
be one of the hive,

Em        Em9         Cmaj7             A7
     will I      choose water over wine      and hold my

Em                    Em9     Cmaj7   A7
own and drive? Oh,        oh, oh.
```

## PRE-CHORUS 2

```
Cmaj7                    A7                          Cmaj7       A7
     It's driven me before, and it seems to be the way that everyone else gets around.

Cmaj7          A7                    Cmaj7       A7
     But lately I'm beginning to find that when I drive myself, my light is found.
```

## *REPEAT CHORUS*

## GUITAR SOLO

```
||: Em          Em9  | Cmaj7      A7   | Em          Em9  | Cmaj7      A7        :||
```

## PRE-CHORUS 3

```
Cmaj7          A7                    Cmaj7   A7                  N.C.
     Would you choose a water over wine?      Hold the wheel and drive.
```

## *REPEAT CHORUS*

## OUTRO

```
Em  Em9     Cmaj7             A7
   Do, do, do,       do, do, do,      do, do, do,

Em    Em9  Cmaj7         A7
   do. No, no,       no. Do, do,    do, do, do.

Em  Em9     Cmaj7             A7
   Do, do, do,       do, do, do,      do, do, do,

Em    Em9  Cmaj7         A7   Cmaj7  A7
   do. No, no,       no, no, no.
```

# How You Remind Me

Words by Chad Kroeger
Music by Nickelback

(Capo 3rd Fret)

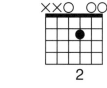 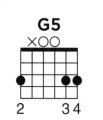 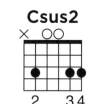 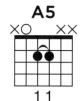

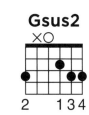 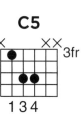 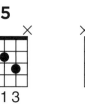 

Asus2    D6sus2    G5    Csus2    A5

Fsus2    Gsus2    C5    D5    Dsus2

## VERSE 1

Moderately

**Asus2**                    **D6sus2  G5**                    **Csus2**
   Never made it as a wise man.    I couldn't cut it as a poor man stealin'.

**Asus2**                    **D6sus2  G5**                                    **Csus2**
   Tired of livin' like a blind man.    I'm sick of sight without a sense of feelin'.

**A5**            **Fsus2**        **Gsus2**
And this is how     you remind me.

**Asus2**        **D6sus2**            **G5**            **Csus2**
   This is how     you remind me of what I really am.

**Asus2**        **D6sus2**            **G5**            **Csus2**
   This is how     you remind me of what I really am.

## CHORUS 1

**A5**                **C5**                **G5**                    **D5**
   It's not like you    to say sorry.    I was waitin' on a different story.

**A5**                **C5**            **G5**                **D5**
   This time I'm    mistaken    for handin' you a heart worth breakin'.

**A5**                    **C5**                **G5**                        **D5**
   And I've been wrong,    I've been down,    been to the bottom of ev'ry bottle.

**A5**                    **C5**            **G5**                **D5**
   These five words in my head    scream, "Are we havin' fun yet?"

**A5**    **D5**    **G5**    **C5**
   Yet,    yet,    yet,    no, no.

**A5**    **D5**    **G5**    **C5**
   Yet,    yet,    yet,    no, no.

## VERSE 2

Asus2                         D6sus2   G5                    Csus2  
   It's not like you didn't know that     I said I love you, and I swear I still do.

Asus2                          D6sus2   G5                      Csus2  
   And it must have been so bad,     'cause livin' with me must've damn near killed you.

Asus2      D6sus2         G5       Csus2  
And this is how       you remind me of what I really am.

Asus2      D6sus2         G5       Csus2  
   This is how       you remind me of what I really am.

## REPEAT CHORUS 1

A5    D5    G5    C5  
   Yet,    yet,    yet,    no, no.

A5    D5    G5    C5  
   Yet,    yet,    yet,    no, no.

## INTERLUDE

| Asus2    Dsus2    | G5        Csus2    | Asus2    Dsus2    | G5        Csus2    ||

## VERSE 3

A5                  Dsus2   G5                Csus2  
   Never made it as a wise man.    I couldn't cut it as a poor man stealin'.

A5           Fsus2       Gsus2  
And this is how      you remind me.

A5           Fsus2       Gsus2  
  This is how      you remind me.

A5           D6sus2       G5       Csus2  
  This is how      you remind me of what I really am.

A5           D6sus2       G5       Csus2  
  This is how      you remind me of what I really am.

## CHORUS 2

```
A5                  C5              G5                    D5
  It's not like you     to say sorry.     I was waitin' on a different story.

A5                  C5          G5 N.C.
  This time I'm      mistaken      for handin' you a heart worth breakin'.

A5                      C5                  G5                        D5
And I've been wrong,      I've been down,      been to the bottom of ev'ry bottle.

A5                  C5              G5                  D5
  These five words in my head      scream, "Are we havin' fun yet?"

A5     C5    G5        D5
  Yet,    yet.     Are we havin' fun yet?

A5     C5    G5        D5
  Yet,    yet.     Are we havin' fun yet?

A5     C5    G5        D5
  Yet,    yet.     Are we havin' fun yet?

A5     C5    Gsus2
  Yet,    yet.          Yet, no.
```

# Learn to Fly

**Words and Music by David Grohl, Oliver Taylor Hawkins and Nate Mendel**

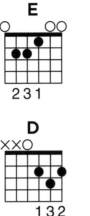
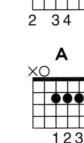
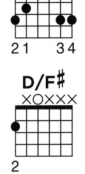
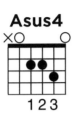

## INTRO

**Moderately**

‖: Bsus4 | F#m11 | E | | :‖

## VERSE 1

Bsus4          F#m11     E
Run and tell all of the angels,     this could take all night.

Bsus4          F#m11           E
Thinkin' it in time will help me get things right.

Bsus4          F#m11      E
Hook me up a new revolution, 'cause this one is a lie.

Bsus4           F#m11         E
I sat around laughing and watched the last one die.

## CHORUS 1

     Bsus4           F#m11    E
Yeah, I'm lookin' to the sky to save me,     lookin' for a sign of life.

Bsus4            F#m11          E
Lookin' for somethin' to help me burn out bright.

    Bsus4        F#m11    E
I'm lookin' for a complication,     lookin' 'cause I'm tired of lyin'.

G                Asus4      A
Make my way back home when I learn to fly

## INTERLUDE

| Bsus4 | F#m11 | E | |  |
|:--|:--|:--|:--|:--|

high.

| Bsus4 | F#m11 | E | |
|:--|:--|:--|:--|

## VERSE 2

Bsus4          F#m11   E
I think I'm dyin' nursing patience,   it can wait one night.

Bsus4          F#m11        E
Give it all away if you give me one last try.

Bsus4          F#m11       E
We'll live happily ever trapped if you just save my life.

Bsus4           F#m11     E
Run and tell the angels that ev'rything's all   right.

## CHORUS 2

Bsus4          F#m11   E
I'm lookin' to the sky to save me,   lookin' for a sign of life.

Bsus4          F#m11        E
Lookin' for somethin' to help me burn out bright.

Bsus4          F#m11   E
I'm lookin' for a complication,   lookin' 'cause I'm tired of tryin'.

G          Asus4   A      E   D/F#
Make my way back home when I learn to fly high.

G          Asus4   A
Make my way back home when I learn to...

## BRIDGE

Bsus4  G         D         E   D/F#
Fly   along with me. I can't quite make it alone.

G          Asus4  A
Try to make this life my own.

Bsus4  G         D         E   D/F#
Fly   along with me. I can't quite make it alone.

G          Asus4  A
Try to make this life my own.

## CHORUS 3

Bsus4               F#m11   E
I'm lookin' to the sky to save me,    lookin' for a sign of life.

Bsus4               F#m11         E
Lookin' for somethin' to help me burn out bright.

       Bsus4          F#m11   E
Yeah, I'm lookin' for a complication,    lookin' 'cause I'm tired of tryin'.

G               Asus4    A
Make my way back home when I learn to...

Bsus4               F#m11   E
Lookin' to the sky to save me,    lookin' for a sign of life.

Bsus4               F#m11         E
Lookin' for somethin' to help me burn out bright.

       Bsus4          F#m11   E
I'm lookin' for a complication,    lookin' 'cause I'm tired of tryin'.

G               Asus4    A       E   D/F#
Make my way back home when I learn to fly high.

G               Asus4    A       E   D/F#
Make my way back home when I learn to fly.

G               Asus4    A
Make my way back home when I learn to...

## OUTRO

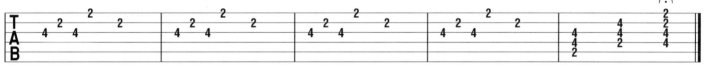

# Hurt

## Words and Music by Trent Reznor

(Capo 2nd Fret)

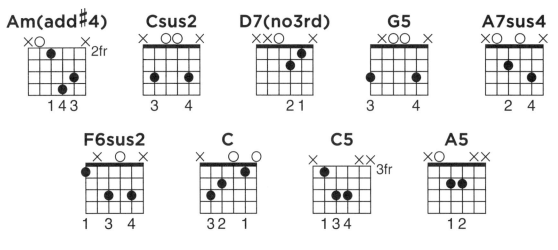

## VERSE 1

Moderately slow

Am(add#4)  Csus2  D7(no3rd)  Am(add#4)    Csus2  D7(no3rd)
I hurt myself today              to see if I            still feel.

Am(add#4)  Csus2  D7(no3rd)          Am(add#4)    Csus2    D7(no3rd)
I focused          on the pain,          the only thing        that's real.

Am(add#4)    Csus2 D7(no3rd)  Am(add#4)    Csus2  D7(no3rd)
The needle tears a hole,          the old familiar sting.

Am(add#4)      Csus2 D7(no3rd)    Am(add#4)        Csus2 D7(no3rd)
Try to kill it all          away            but I remember  ev'rything.

## INTERLUDE 1

| G5 | | A7sus4 | | F6sus2 | | C | | |
| G5 | | A7sus4 | | F6sus2 | | C | | |

## CHORUS 1

G5  A7sus4      F6sus2  C
What have I become,        my sweetest friend?

G5  A7sus4    F6sus2      C
Ev'ryone I know goes away in the end.

G5    A7sus4        F6sus2  G5
And you could have it all,      my empire of dirt.

    A7sus4      F6sus2  G5
I will let you down,      I will make you hurt.

## INTERLUDE 2

‖: Am(add♯4)　　　　　　　　　　│ Csus2　　　　　D7(no3rd)　　　　　:‖

## VERSE 2

Am(add♯4)　Csus2　　D7(no3rd)　Am(add♯4)　Csus2　D7(no3rd)
　　　　I wear this crown of shit　　　　　upon my liar's chair

Am(add♯4)　Csus2　　D7(no3rd)　　　Am(add♯4)　Csus2　D7(no3rd)
　　　　full of broken thoughts　　　　　I cannot　　　　repair.

Am(add♯4)　　Csus2　　　D7(no3rd)　Am(add♯4)　　Csus2　　D7(no3rd)
　　　Beneath the stains of time　　　　　the feelings disappear.

Am(add♯4)　Csus2　　D7(no3rd)　Am(add♯4)　Csus2　D7(no3rd)
　　　You are someone else,　　　　I am  still right here.

## CHORUS 2

G5　A7sus4　　　　　F6sus2　C
What have I become,　　　my sweetest friend?

G5　A7sus4　　　F6sus2　　　C
Ev'ryone I know goes away in the end.

G5　　A7sus4　　　　F6sus2　G5
And you could have it all,　　my empire of dirt.

　　A7sus4　　　F6sus2　G5
　　I will let you down,　　I will make you hurt.

　　A7sus4　　　F6sus2　G5
　　If I could start again　　a million miles away,

　　A7sus4　　　F6sus2　G5　　C5　　A5
　　I would keep myself,　　I would find a way.

19

# I Will Follow You into the Dark

Words and Music by Benjamin Gibbard

(Capo 5th Fret)

| Am | C | F | Gadd4/B |
|---|---|---|---|
|  | | 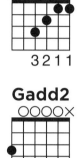 | 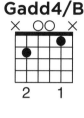 |
| 2 3 1 | 3 2  1 | 3 2 1 1 | 2   1 |

| G5 | E | Gadd2 | Fm |
|---|---|---|---|
| | | | |
| 3      4 | 2 3 1 | 3 | 3 1 1 1 |

## INTRO

Moderately fast

| Am | C | F | C      Gadd4/B |
| Am | C | G5 | |
| Am | C | E | Am      Gadd2 |
| F | Fm | C | |

## VERSE 1

C               Am
Love of mine, someday you will die,

       F                 C       G5
but I'll be close behind. I'll follow you into the dark.

     C                Am
No blinding light or tunnels to gates of white,

       F                 C       G5
just our hands clasped so tight waiting for the hint of a spark.

## CHORUS 1

  Am             C           F       C  Gadd4/B
If heaven and hell decide that they both are satisfied,

  Am         C      G5
illuminate the no's on their vacancy signs.

  Am            C          E    Am  Gadd2
If there's no one beside you when your soul embarks,

       F    Fm        C
then I'll follow you into the dark.

## VERSE 2

    C                        Am  
In Cath'lic school, as vicious as Roman rule,

          F              C      G5  
I got my knuckles bruised by a lady in black.

    C                    Am  
And I held my tongue as she told me, "Son,

        F             C      G5  
fear is the heart of love." So I never went back.

## REPEAT CHORUS 1

## VERSE 3

C                      Am  
You and me, have seen everything to see from Bankok to

F          C        G5  
Calgary, and the soles of your shoes

  C                Am  
are all worn down. The time for sleep is now, but it's nothing to

F            C        G5    Am  
cry about 'cause we'll hold each other soon in the blackest of rooms.

| F | | | |

## CHORUS 2

 Am             C           F      C  Gadd4/B  
If heaven and hell decide that they both are satisfied,

 Am       C       G5  
illuminate the no's on their vacancy signs.

 Am            C           E    Am  Gadd2  
If there's no one beside you when your soul embarks,

F     Fm           C  Gadd4/B  Am  
I'll follow you into the dark.

    F      Fm         C  
And I'll follow you unto the dark.

# Lightning Crashes

Words and Music by Edward Kowalczyk, Chad Taylor,
Patrick Dahlheimer and Chad Gracey

(Capo 2nd Fret)

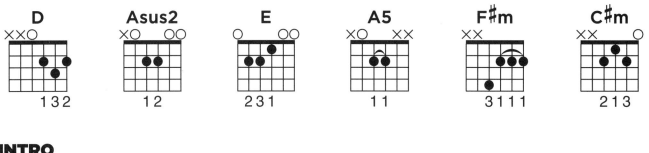

## INTRO

Moderately

‖: D | Asus2 | E | | :‖

## VERSE 1

D       Asus2       E
Lightning crashes, a new mother cries.

D       Asus2       E
Her placenta falls to the floor.

D   Asus2       E
The angel opens her eyes. The confusion sets in

D       Asus2       E
before the doctor can even close the door.

## VERSE 2

D       Asus2       E
Lightning crashes, an old mother dies.

D       Asus2       E
Her intentions fall to the floor.

D   Asus2       E
The angel closes her eyes. The confusion that was hers

D       Asus2       E
belongs now to the baby down the hall.

## CHORUS 1

D   A5   E
Oh, I feel it coming back again

D   A5   E
like a rolling thunder chasing the wind.

D   A5       E
Forces pulling from the center of the earth again.

D   A5   E
I can feel it.

## VERSE 2

D     Asus2       E
Lightning crashes, a new mother cries.

D   Asus2       E
This moment she's been waiting for.

D  Asus2      E
The angel opens her eyes, pale blue colored

 D       Asus2      E
i - ris presents the circle, puts the glory out to hide, hide.


## REPEAT CHORUS 1

D   A5  E
I can feel it.


## BRIDGE

**Play 3 times**

‖: F#m      | C#m       :‖ D       | E      ‖
                                  Oh,

F#m  C#m     F#m  C#m    D  E
 I, oh, oo, oo, I, I, I.   Oh, oo, oo, I, I, I,  I, I.


## CHORUS 2

D   A5  E
I can feel it coming back again

D   A5   E
like a rolling thunder chasing the wind.

D    A5     E
Forces pulling from the center of the earth again.

D   A5 E
I can feel it.


## REPEAT CHORUS 2 (2 TIMES)

 D   A5 E
I can feel it.

D   A5 E
I can feel it.

rit.
| D      Asus2  | E          ‖

# Lonely Boy

**Words and Music by Dan Auerbach, Patrick Carney and Brian Burton**

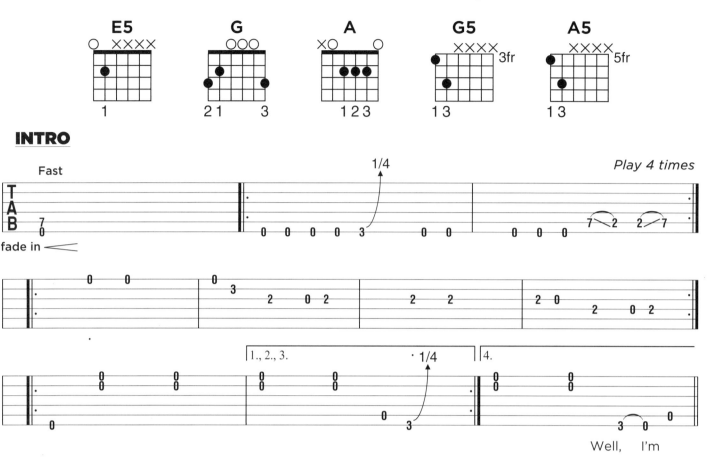

## INTRO

*Fast*     *Play 4 times*

Well, I'm

## VERSE 1

E5        G   A
so above you, and it's plain to see,

   E5        G   A
but I came to love you anyway.

     E5        G     A
So you pulled my heart out, and I don't mind bleeding

E5                 G     A
any old time you keep me waiting,    waiting, waiting.

## CHORUS

E5      G5           A5
Oh, oh, oh,   I got a love that keeps me waiting.

E5   G5           A5
Oh, oh,   I got a love that keeps me waiting.

E5           G5          A5
  I'm a lonely boy.     I'm a lonely boy.

E5      G5           A5
Oh, oh, oh,   I got a love that keeps me waiting.

## INTERLUDE

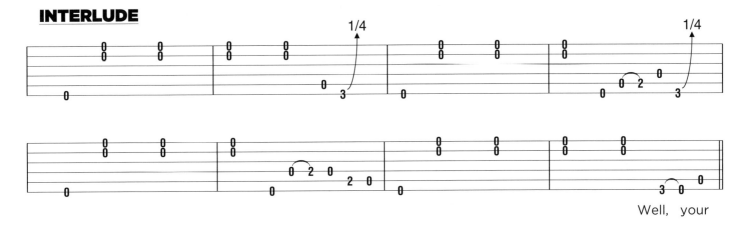

Well, your

## VERSE 2

E5                                    G        A
mama kept you, but your daddy left you,

    E5                                      G    A
and I should have done you just the same.

    E5                    G          A
But I came to love you. Am I born to bleed

E5                                G       A
any old time you keep me waiting,    waiting, waiting?

## *REPEAT CHORUS*

## INTERLUDE

*Play 4 times*

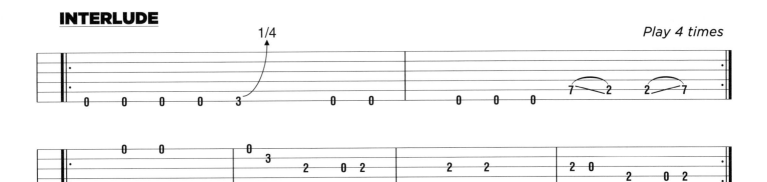

## *REPEAT CHORUS*

# Losing My Religion

**Words and Music by William Berry, Peter Buck, Michael Mills and Michael Stipe**

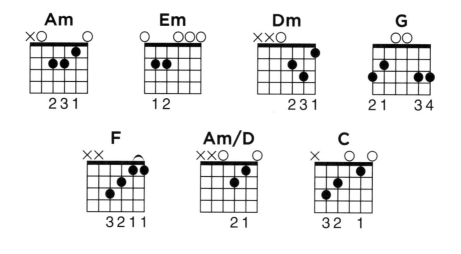

## INTRO

Moderately fast

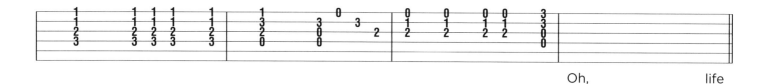

Oh,                                                                        life

## VERSE 1

**Am**                **Em**
     is bigger,     it's bigger than you,

              **Am**                         **Em**
and you are not     me. The lengths that I will go to. The distance in your eyes.

**Am**  **Em**
     Oh, no I've said too much.

**Dm**          **G**
     I set it up.

## VERSE 2

                **Am**                  **Em**
That's me in the corner. That's me in the spotlight,

              **Am**             **Em**
losing my religion, trying to keep up with you.

            **Am**               **Em**
And I don't know if I can do it.     Oh, no, I've said too much.

**Dm**           **G**
     I haven't said enough.

## CHORUS 1

                                    **F**            **Dm**            **G**           **Am**
I thought that I heard you laughing. I thought that I heard you sing.

 **F**                   **Dm G**    **Am**     **G**
I think I thought I saw    you try.

## VERSE 3

              **Am**                  **Em**
Every whisper of ev'ry waking hour I'm choosing my

          **Am**            **Em**
confessions, trying to keep an eye on you,

           **Am**                 **Em**
like a hurt lost and blinded fool, fool.     Oh, no, I've said too much.

**Dm**            **G**
   I set it up.

## VERSE 4

              **Am**                **Em**
Consider this. Consider this the hint of the century.

              **Am**            **Em**
Consider this the slip that brought me to my knees, failed.

**Am**                      **Em**
What if all these fantasies come flailing around?

         **Dm**        **G**
Now I've said too much.

## *REPEAT CHORUS 1*

## INTERLUDE

| **Am** | | **G** | | **F** | | **G** | |
|---|---|---|---|---|---|---|---|

But

| **C** | | **Am/D** | | **C** | | **Am/D** |
|---|---|---|---|---|---|---|

that was just a dream.                                That was just a dream.

## *REPEAT VERSE 2*

## CHORUS 2

                                    **F**         **Dm**             **G**           **Am**
I thought that I heard you laughing. I thought that I heard you sing.

 **F**               **Dm** **G**     **Am**
I think I thought I saw    you try.

       **F**                 **Dm** **G**  **Am**
But that was just a dream.     Try, cry. Why try?

**F**                   **Dm**  **G**       **Am**            **G**
That was just a dream,  just a dream,  just a dream, dream.

## OUTRO

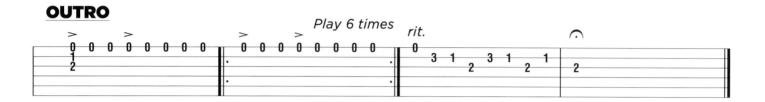

# Santeria

### Words and Music by Brad Nowell, Eric Wilson and Floyd Gaugh

(Capo 4th Fret)

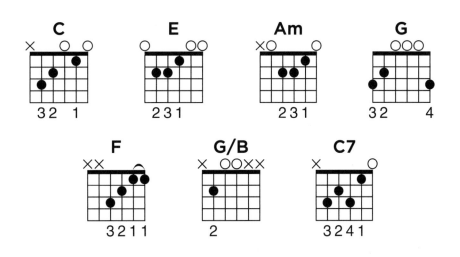

## INTRO

Moderately slow

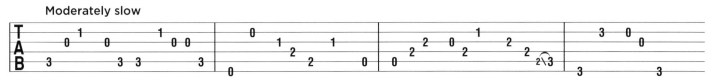

## VERSE 1

```
        C                      E
I don't practice santeria, I ain't got no crystal ball.

     Am                  G
Well, I had a million dollars but I,   I'd spend it all.

     C                          E
If I could find that heina and that Sancho that she's found,

        Am                       G
well, I'd pop a cap in Sancho and I'd slap her down.
```

## CHORUS 1

```
F    G           C  G/B  Am
  But I really wanna know,      ah, baby, mm.

F    G           C  G/B  Am
  All I really wanna say   I      can't define.

F     G           C  G/B  Am     F    G
  Well, it's love that I need.       Oh,    my soul will have to
```

## VERSE 2

C      E
wait 'til I get back, find a heina of my own.

Am       G
Daddy's gonna love one and all.

 C       E
I feel the break, feel the break, feel the break and I got to live it out,

Am   G
  oh, yeah, huh. Well, I swear that I,

## CHORUS 2

F  G    C G/B Am
  well I really wanna know,   ah, baby.

F  G   C G/B Am
  All I really wanna say I  can't define.

F  G    C G/B Am F    G
  Got love, make it go.     Well, my soul will have to...

## GUITAR SOLO

‖: C    | E    | Am   

1.
| G    :‖

2.
| G      ‖
         Oo,

## CHORUS 3

F  G    C G/B Am
  all I really wanna say,   ah, baby.

F  G    C G/B Am
  What I really wanna say is  I've got

F   G     C G/B  Am F  G
  mine and I'll make it. Oo, yes, I'm coming up.  Tell Sanchito that if he

## VERSE 3

C        E
  knows what is good for him, he best go run and hide.

Am       G
Daddy's got a new forty-five

  C        E
and I won't think twice to stick that barrel straight down Sancho's throat.

 Am       G
Believe me when I say that I got something for his punk ass.

## CHORUS 4

```
   F        G              C  G/B  Am
   What I really wanna know,    ah, baby.

   F        G              C  G/B  Am
   Oo, what I really wanna say   is    there's just

   F        G              C  G/B  Am        F    G
   one way back and I'll make       it. Yeah,   my soul will have to

   C    G/B  Am  G  F  G  C7
   rit.
   wait.
```

# Mr. Brightside

Words and Music by Brandon Flowers, Dave Keuning,
Mark Stoermer and Ronnie Vannucci

(Capo 4th Fret)

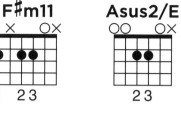
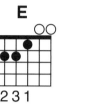

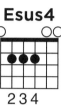

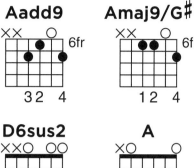

## INTRO

Moderately

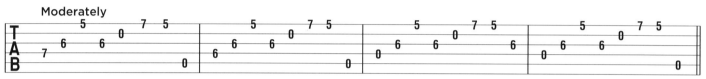

## VERSE

**Aadd9**                                    **Amaj9/G♯**
   1. Comin'⎫
   2. I'm comin'⎭ outta my cage and I've been doin' just

**Dmaj13**
fine. Gotta, gotta be down because I want it all.

**Aadd9**                                    **Amaj9/G♯**
   It started out with a kiss. How did it end up like

**Dmaj13**
this? It was only a kiss, it was only a kiss.

**Aadd9**                                    **Amaj9/G♯**
   Now I'm falling asleep, and she's calling a cab

**Dmaj13**
     while he's having a smoke and she's takin' a drag.

**Aadd9**                                    **Amaj9/G♯**
   Now they're goin' to bed and my stomach is sick.

**Dmaj13**
   And it's all in my head, but she's touching his

## PRE-CHORUS

F#m11               Asus2/E       D6sus2

chest. Now he takes off her dress. Now let me go.

F#m11                    Asus2/E     D6sus2

{ And }
{ 'Cause } I just can't look; it's killing me and taking control.

## CHORUS

A     Dsus2       F#m11     E

Jealousy, turning saints into the sea. Swimming through sick

A     Dsus2       F#m11   E

lullabies, choking on your alibis,    but it's just the

A     Dsus2     F#m11      E

price I pay. Destiny is calling me. Open up my

A      Dsus2   F#m11             E

eager eyes         'cause I'm Mister Brightside.

## INTERLUDE 1

‖: A              | Dsus2          | F#m11         | E        :‖

## *REPEAT VERSE*

## *REPEAT PRE-CHORUS*

## *REPEAT CHORUS*

## INTERLUDE 2

                                                         1.                    2.

‖: A              | Dsus2          | F#m11         | E      :‖ E         ‖

## OUTRO

                                                           1., 2., 3.             4.

‖: A              | Dsus2          | F#m11         | E          :‖ E   Esus4   E     ‖

never.

# No Rain

## Words and Music by Blind Melon

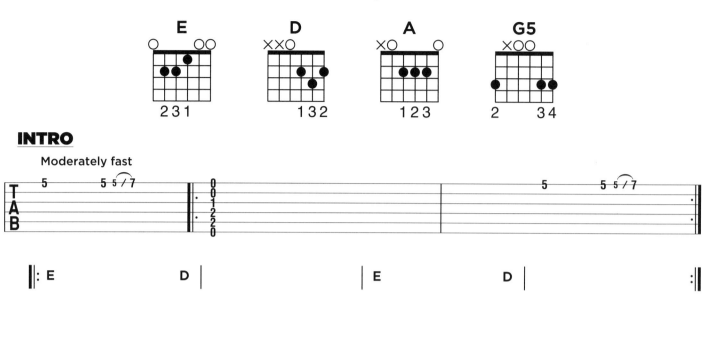

## INTRO

**Moderately fast**

```
      5      5 5/7                  0                           5      5 5/7
T ─────────────────────││:─────0──────────────│──────────────│───────────────────────:│
A ─────────────────────││:─────1──────────────│──────────────│───────────────────────:│
B ─────────────────────││:─────2──────────────│──────────────│───────────────────────:│
                       ││:─────2──────────────│──────────────│───────────────────────:│
                       ││:─────0──────────────│──────────────│───────────────────────:│
```

‖: E              D  |              | E        D  |  :‖

## CHORUS 1

E                         D
All I can say is that my life is pretty plain;

  A                            G5      E
I like watchin' the puddles gather rain.

                      D
And all I can do is just pour some tea for two

    A                        G5      E
and speak my point of view, but it's not sane. It's not sane.

## VERSE 1

E        D        E        D
I just want someone to say to me, oh, oh, oh, oh.

E        D              E     D
"I'll always be there when you wake."    Oh, yeah.

E              D              E        D
Ya know I'd like to keep my cheeks dry today, hey.

E              D              E        D
So stay with me and I'll have it made. (I'll have it made.)

## CHORUS 2

      E                      D
And I don't understand why I sleep all day

       A                G5      E
and I start to complain that there's no rain.

                           D
And all I can do is read a book to stay awake.

       A                  G5      E
And it rips my life away, but it's a great escape, escape, escape, escape.

## GUITAR SOLO

*Play 4 times*

‖: E             D |               | E          D | :‖

## CHORUS 3

   E                    D
All I can say is that my life is pretty plain;

       A                G5            E
You don't like my point of view; you think that I'm insane. It's not sane. It's not sane.

## VERSE 2

   E      D          E        D
I just want someone to say to me, oh, oh, oh, oh.

   E         D              E   D
"I'll always be there when you wake."    Oh, yeah.

   E              D          E        D
Ya know I'd like to keep my cheeks dry today, hey.

   E         D            E          D
So stay with me and I'll have it made.        Oh, oh,    and I'll have it made.
                                   (I'll have it    made.)

## OUTRO

   E         D              E         D
            Oo, and I'll have it made.     Oh!     Lord, no, no.
   (I'll have it made.                I'll have it  made.)

   E                 D                 E         D
    Ya know I'm real - ly gonna,   really gonna have it made.     Yeah!     Ya know I'll have it made.
    (I'll      have it     made.                          I'll have it  made.)

   E         D       E         D
   (I'll have it made.) Oh.    (I'll have it made.) Oh.

   E         D       E         D
   (I'll have it made.) Oh.    (I'll have it made.) Oh.

   N.C.
     Oh, oh, oh, oh, oh.

# One Week

Words and Music by Ed Robertson

(Capo 2nd Fret)

**G5**

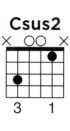

**Cadd9**

**G**

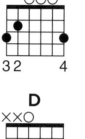

**C**

**Csus2**

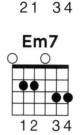

**Em7**

**D**

**Bm7**

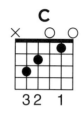

## CHORUS 1

Moderately

     G5                               Cadd9
It's been one week since you looked at me,

G5                                   Cadd9
cocked your head to the side and said, "I'm angry."

G5                             Cadd9
Five days since you laughed at me,

     G5                             Cadd9
saying, "Get that together and come back and see me."

G5                        Cadd9
Three days since the living room.

     G5                           Cadd9
I realized it's all my fault, but couldn't tell you.

G5                Cadd9
Yesterday you'd forgiven me,

     G5                   Cadd9
but it'll still be two days till I say I'm sorry.

## VERSE 1

G     C    Csus2
Hold it now and watch the hoodwink

      G    C     Csus2
as I make you stop, think. You'll think you're looking at Aquaman.

G     C    Csus2
I summon fish to the dish, although I like the chalet

G      C    Csus2
Swiss. I like the sushi 'cause it's never touched a frying pan.

G     C   Csus2
Hot, like wasabi, when I bust rhymes.

      G    C   Csus2
Big, like LeAnn Rimes, because I'm all about value.

G      C   Csus2
Bert Kaempfort's got the mad hits.

      G    C   Csus2
You try to match wits. You try to hold me, but I bust through.

G       C   Csus2
Gonna make a break and take a fake. I'd like a stinking, aching

G     C   Csus2
shake. I like vanilla, it's the finest of the flavors.

G       C     Csus2
Gotta see the show, 'cause then you'll know the vertigo is gonna

G      C   Csus2
grow, 'cause it's so dangerous you'll have to sign a waiver.

## PRE-CHORUS 1

Em7     D
How can I help it if I think you're funny when you're mad?

Bm7   Cadd9
Trying hard not to smile, though I feel bad.

Em7     D
I'm the kind of guy who laughs at a funeral.

Bm7    Cadd9
Can't understand what I mean, well, you soon will.

Em7     D
I have the tendency to wear my mind on my sleeve.

Bm7   Cadd9
I have a history of taking off my shirt.

## CHORUS 2

G5                                      Cadd9
It's been one week since you looked at me,

G5                                            Cadd9
threw your arms in the air and said, "You're crazy."

G5                              Cadd9
Five days since you tackled me.

G5                               Cadd9
I've still got the rugburns on both knees.

G5                               Cadd9
It's been three days since the afternoon

G5                                    Cadd9
you realized it's not my fault, not a moment too soon.

G5                    Cadd9
Yesterday you'd forgiven me,

G5                                    Cadd9
and now I sit back and wait till you say you're sorry.


## INTERLUDE

‖: G     C     Csus2 | G     C     Csus2 | G     C     Csus2 | G     C     Csus2 :‖


## VERSE 2

G             C       Csus2
Chickity China, the Chinese chicken.

G             C       Csus2
You have a drumstick and your brain stops ticking.

G             C       Csus2
Watching X Files with no lights on,

G        C       Csus2
we're dans la maison. I hope the Smoking Man's in this one.

G             C       Csus2
Like Harrison Ford, I'm getting frantic.

G         C       Csus2
Like Sting, I'm tantric. Like Snickers, guaranteed to satisfy.

G             C       Csus2
Like Kurosawa, I make mad films.

G         C       Csus2
'Kay, I don't make films, but if I did they'd have a samurai.

G             C       Csus2
Gonna get a set of better clubs. Gonna find the kind with tiny

G             C       Csus2
nubs, just so my irons aren't always flying off the backswing.

G             C       Csus2
Gonna get in tune with Sailor Moon, 'cause that cartoon has got the

G             C       Csus2
boom anime babes that make me think the wrong thing.

## PRE-CHORUS 2

Em7                  D
How can I help it if I think you're funny when you're mad?

Bm7        Cadd9
Trying hard not to smile, though I feel bad.

Em7             D
I'm the kind of guy who laughs at a funeral.

Bm7        Cadd9
Can't understand what I mean, you soon will.

Em7             D
I have the tendency to wear my mind on my sleeve.

Bm7        Cadd9
I have a history of losing my shirt.

## CHORUS 3

        G5                                 Cadd9
It's been one week since you looked at me,

G5                                 Cadd9
dropped your arms to the side and said, "I'm sorry."

G5                     Cadd9
Five days since I laughed at you and said,

G5                     Cadd9
"You just did just what I thought you were gonna do."

G5                     Cadd9
Three days since the living room.

   G5                                Cadd9
We realized we were both to blame but what could we do?

G5                     Cadd9
Yesterday you just smiled at me,

     G5                          Cadd9
'cause it'll still be two days till we say we're sorry.

## OUTRO

G   C   Csus2   G             C     Csus2
                      It'll still be two days till we say we're sorry.

G   C   Csus2   G             C     Csus2
                      It'll still be two days till we say we're sorry.

G   C   Csus2   G             C     Csus2
                      Birchmount Stadium, home of the Robbie.

| G | C | Csus2 | G | C | Csus2 | G |
|---|---|-------|---|---|-------|---|

# Plush

**Words and Music by Eric Kretz, Robert DeLeo, Dean DeLeo and Scott Weiland**

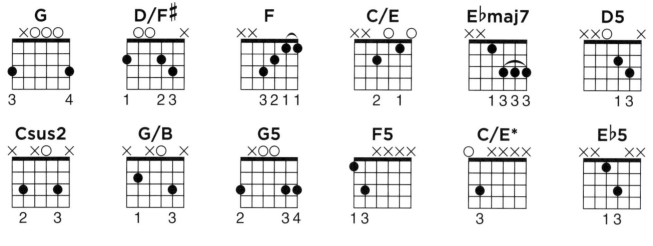

## INTRO

**Moderately**

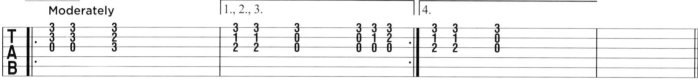

## VERSE 1

G    D/F♯  F              C/E  E♭maj7            F

And I feel that time's a wasted go,         so where you going to

G               D/F♯  F          C/E  E♭maj7          F

tomorrow? And I see that these are lies to come,     so would you even care?

## PRE-CHORUS 1

D5  Csus2  G/B  Csus2     D5  Csus2  G/B  Csus2

          And I feel  it,

D5  Csus2  G/B  Csus2     D5  Csus2  G/B  Csus2

          And I feel  it,

## CHORUS

E♭maj7               F

    Where you goin' for tomorrow?

E♭maj7                 F

    Where you goin' with a mask I found?

E♭maj7                    F

    And I feel, and I feel when the dogs begin to smell her,

E♭maj7         F

    will she smell alone?

## INTERLUDE

```
|-----------------------|---------------------|-------------------||
|-3--3----3-------------|-3--3----3-----------|-------------------||
|-3--3----3-------------|-1--1----0-----------|-------------------||
|-3--3----2-------------|-1--1----0-----------|-------------------||
|-3--3----3-------------|-2--2----0-----------|-------------------||
|-0--0----3-------------|-2--2----0-----------|-------------------||
```

## VERSE 2

| G | D/F♯ | F | | C/E | E♭maj7 | F |
|---|------|---|---|-----|--------|---|

And I feel so much depends on the weather,   so is it raining in your

| G | D/F♯ | F | | C/E | E♭maj7 | F |
|---|------|---|---|-----|--------|---|

bedroom? And I see   that these are the eyes of disarray,   would you even care?

## PRE-CHORUS 2

D5  Csus2  G/B  Csus2   D5  Csus2  G/B  Csus2

And I feel   it,

D5  Csus2  G/B  Csus2   D5  Csus2  G/B  Csus2

And she feels  it,

## *REPEAT CHORUS*

## BRIDGE

G5            F5         C/E*        E♭5      D5

When the dogs do find her,   got time, time to wait for

G5     F5      C/E*        E♭5      D5

tomorrow,   to find it,   to find it,   to find   it.

G5            F5         C/E*        E♭5      D5

When the dogs do find her,   got time, time to wait for

G5     F5      C/E*        E♭5      D5

tomorrow,   to find it,   to find it,   to find   it.

## *REPEAT INTRO*

## *REPEAT CHORUS*

## *REPEAT BRIDGE*

## OUTRO

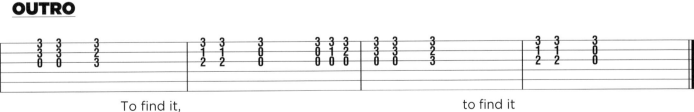

```
|------------------|------------------|------------------|------------------|
|-3--3----3--------|-3--3----3--------|-3--3-3--3--3-----|-3--3----3--------|
|-3--3----3--------|-1--1----0--------|-3--3-3--3--3-----|-1--1----0--------|
|-3--3----2--------|-1--1----0--------|-0--1-2--3--3-----|-1--1----0--------|
|-3--3----3--------|-2--2----0--------|-0--0-0--0--3-----|-2--2----0--------|
|-0--0----3--------|-2--2----0--------|-0--0-0-----3-----|-2--2----0--------|
```

To find it,                              to find it

# Say It Ain't So

## Words and Music by Rivers Cuomo

(Capo 3rd Fret)

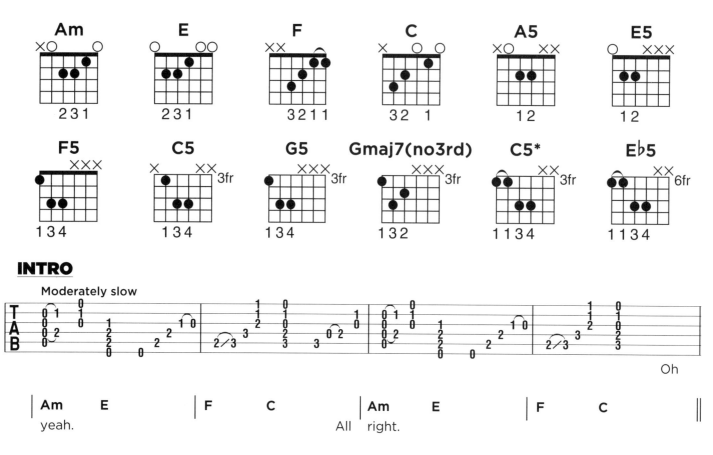

## INTRO

Moderately slow

Oh

| Am | E | F | C | Am | E | F | C ‖ |
|----|---|---|---|-----|---|---|-----|

yeah.      All   right.

## VERSE 1

Am        E     F      C
Somebody's Heinee is crowdin' my icebox.

Am        E     F      C
Somebody's cold one is givin' me chills.

Am        E      F   C
Guess I'll just close my eyes.     Oh

## INTERLUDE 1

| Am | E | F | C | Am | E | F | C ‖ |
|----|---|---|---|-----|---|---|-----|

yeah.      All   right.      Feels   good      in - side.

## VERSE 2

Am      E   F      C
Flip on the tele', wrestle with Jimmy.

Am      E   F      C
Something is bubblin' behind my back.

     Am   E   F     C
The bottle is ready to blow.

## CHORUS

```
A5  E5  F5        C5  A5      E5    F5        C5
    Say it ain't so.     Your drug is a heartbreaker.

A5  E5  F5        C5  A5      E5    F5    C5
    Say it ain't so.     My love is a life taker.
```

## INTERLUDE 2

```
| Am      E          | F      C          | Am      E          | F      C          ‖
```

## VERSE 3

```
Am      E      F      C
I can't confront you. I never could do

Am            E        F        C
that which might hurt you, so try and be cool when I say

Am    E    F                  C
    this way is a water slide away from me that takes you further every

Am  E      F      C
day.    So be cool.
```

## REPEAT CHORUS

## BRIDGE

```
G5            Gmaj7(no3rd)   C5*        Eb5
    Dear Daddy,      I write you     in spite of years of silence.

G5                Gmaj7(no3rd)      C5*            Eb5
    You've cleaned up,      found Jesus,     things are good or so I hear.

G5        Gmaj7(no3rd)   C5*      Eb5
    This bottle      of Steven's     awakens ancient feelings.

G5            Gmaj7(no3rd)    C5*      Eb5
    Like father,      step father,     the son is drowning in the.

A5    E5      F5        C5
flood,    yeah,    yeah, yeah, yeah, yeah.
```

## GUITAR SOLO

```
| Am   E      | F    C          | Am   E      | F    C          | Am   E      | F    C          ‖
```

## REPEAT CHORUS

## REPEAT INTRO

# Seven Nation Army

### Words and Music by Jack White

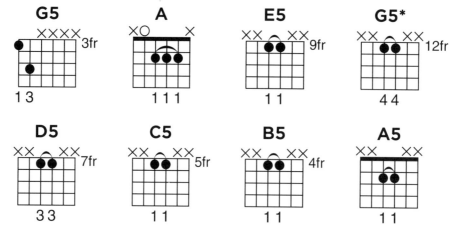

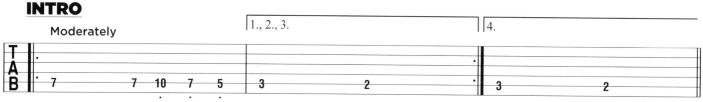

**INTRO**

Moderately

I'm gonna

**VERSE 1**

fight 'em off,     a seven nation   army couldn't hold me back.     They're gonna

rip it off,     taking their   time  right  behind my back.     And  I'm

talking to myself at night   because I can't forget.

Back and forth through my mind   behind a cigarette.     And the

G5                    A

message coming from my eyes says leave it alone.

## INTERLUDE

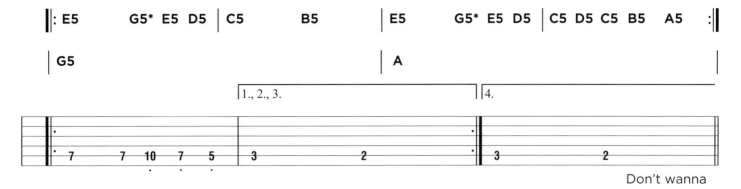

‖: E5      G5* E5 D5 | C5      B5      | E5      G5* E5 D5 | C5 D5 C5 B5    A5    :‖

| G5                      | A

Don't wanna

## VERSE 2

hear about it,           ev'ry single one's got a stor - y to tell.      Ev'ryone

knows about it,           from the Queen of England to the hounds of hell.      And if I

catch it coming back my way    I'm gonna serve it to you.                And

that ain't what you want to hear,    but that's what I'll do.              And the

**G5**                    **A**
feeling coming from my bones says find a home.

## GUITAR SOLO

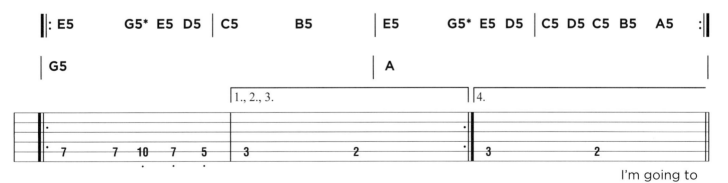

‖: E5      G5* E5 D5 | C5      B5      | E5      G5* E5 D5 | C5 D5 C5 B5    A5    :‖

| G5                      | A

I'm going to

## VERSE 3

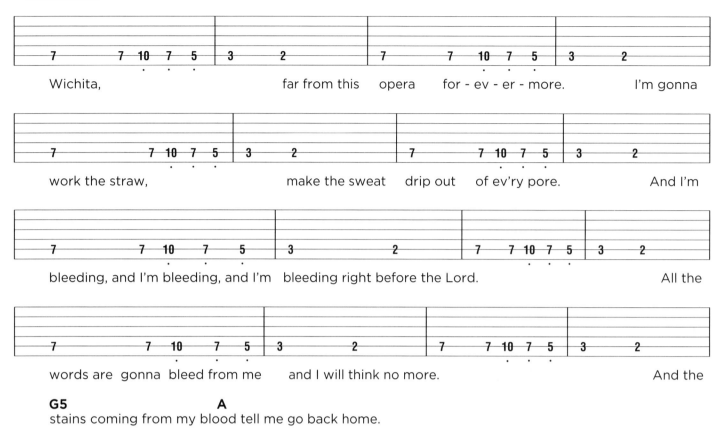

```
7           7  10  7  5 | 3        2    | 7           7  10  7  5 | 3        2
              .   .  .                                   .   .  .
```

Wichita,                    far from this  opera   for - ev - er - more.            I'm gonna

```
7           7  10  7  5 | 3        2    | 7           7  10  7  5 | 3        2
              .   .  .                                   .   .  .
```

work the straw,                make the sweat   drip out   of ev'ry pore.            And I'm

```
7           7  10    7     5 | 3          2       | 7     7  10  7  5 | 3      2
              .       .     .                                 .   .  .
```

bleeding, and I'm bleeding, and I'm   bleeding right before the Lord.                All the

```
7           7  10    7     5 | 3          2       | 7     7  10  7  5 | 3      2
              .       .     .                                 .   .  .
```

words are  gonna  bleed from me      and I will think no more.                And the

**G5**                          **A**
stains coming from my blood tell me go back home.


## OUTRO

‖: **E5**        **G5\* E5 D5** | **C5**        **B5**      | **E5**        **G5\* E5 D5** | **C5 D5 C5 B5   A5**    :‖

| **E5**                                                    |

# Smells Like Teen Spirit

### Words and Music by Kurt Cobain, Dave Grohl and Krist Novoselic

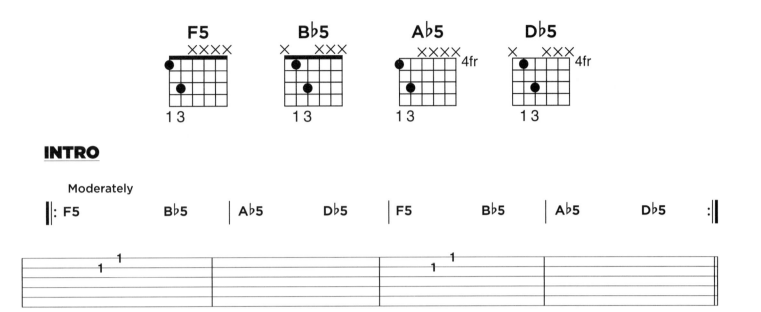

## INTRO

Moderately

‖: F5      Bb5 | Ab5      Db5 | F5      Bb5 | Ab5      Db5 :‖

## VERSE 1

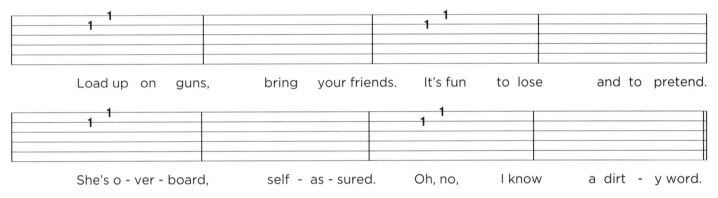

Load up on guns,    bring your friends. It's fun   to lose     and to pretend.

She's o - ver - board,    self - as - sured. Oh, no,    I know    a dirt - y word.

## PRE-CHORUS

F5    Bb5   Ab5   Db5
Hello, hello, hello, how low?

F5    Bb5   Ab5   Db5
Hello, hello, hello, how low?

F5    Bb5   Ab5   Db5
Hello, hello, hello, how low?

F5    Bb5   Ab5   Db5
Hello, hello, hello.

## CHORUS

             **F5**      **B♭5**          **A♭5**     **D♭5**
With the lights out     it's less dang'rous.

           **F5**      **B♭5**     **A♭5**   **D♭5**
Here we are now,     entertain us.

        **F5**   **B♭5**       **A♭5**    **D♭5**
I feel stupid    and contagious.

          **F5**      **B♭5**     **A♭5**   **D♭5**
Here we are now,     entertain us.

        **F5**  **B♭5**       **A♭5**   **D♭5**
A mullato,    an albino,

        **F5**  **B♭5**       **A♭5**   **D♭5**
a mosquito,    my libido.    Yeah.

## INTERLUDE 1

Hey.                        Yay.

## VERSE 2

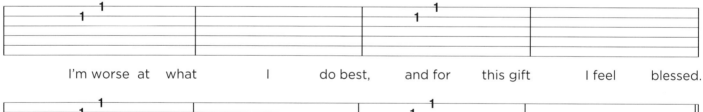

I'm worse at  what      I     do best,   and for   this gift   I feel    blessed.

Our lit - tle group    has al - ways been   and al - ways will   until   the end.

## *REPEAT PRE-CHORUS*

## *REPEAT CHORUS*

## INTERLUDE 2

Hey.

Yay.

## GUITAR SOLO

$\|$: F5      B♭5  |  A♭5      D♭5  |  F5      B♭5  |  A♭5      D♭5  :$\|$

## INTERLUDE 3

## VERSE 3

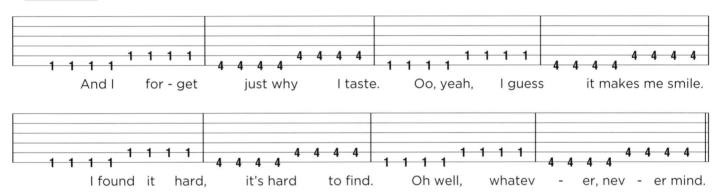

And I   for - get    just why   I taste.    Oo, yeah,   I guess    it makes me smile.

I found   it   hard,    it's hard    to find.    Oh well,    whatev  -  er, nev - er mind.

## *REPEAT PRE-CHORUS*

## *REPEAT CHORUS*

## OUTRO

      F5   B♭5     A♭5   D♭5
a denial,     a denial,

      F5   B♭5     A♭5   D♭5
a denial,     a denial,

      F5   B♭5     A♭5   D♭5
a denial,     a denial,

      F5   B♭5     A♭5   D♭5     F5
a denial,     a denial,     a denial,

# Under the Bridge

Words and Music by Anthony Kiedis, Flea, John Frusciante and Chad Smith

(Capo 2nd Fret)

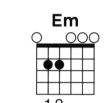

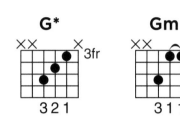
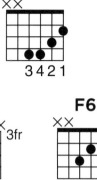
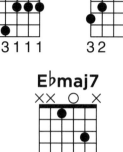
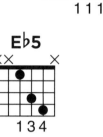
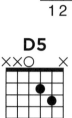

## INTRO

Moderately

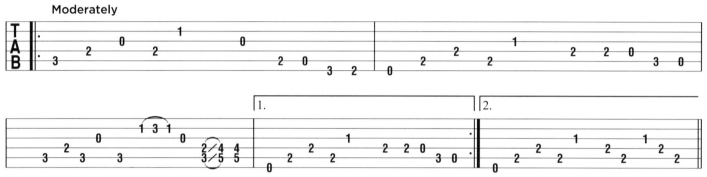

## VERSE 1

D      A     Bm     F♯m   G
Sometimes I feel like I don't have a part - ner.

D      A     Bm     G
Sometimes I feel like my only friend

     D   A     Bm   F♯m   G
is the city I live in, the city of an - gels.

D      A     Bm     G   Dmaj7
Lonely as I am, together we cry.

## VERSE 2

D      A     Bm     F♯m   G
I drive on her streets 'cause she's my compan - ion.

D      A     Bm     G
I walk through her hills 'cause she knows who I am.

    D     A     Bm   F♯m   G
She sees my good deeds and she kisses me wind - y.

D   A     Bm     G   Dmaj7
I never worry. Now that is a lie.

## CHORUS 1

        Em         D       A    Em  
I don't ever want to feel    like I did that day.

                    D     A     Em  
Take me to the place I love,    take me all the way.

              D     A     Em  
I don't ever want to feel    like I did that day.

                    D     A      Em  
Take me to the place I love,    take me all the way,

## INTERLUDE 1

| D       A            | Bm  F#m   G | D        A        | Bm     G  
         yeah,           yeah,  yeah.

## VERSE 3

      D         A            Bm   F#m  G  
It's hard to believe that there's nobody out    there.

      D         A     Bm    G  
It's hard to believe that I'm all alone.

      D         A          Bm    F#m  G  
At least I have her love, the city, she loves  me.

  D        A     Bm       G  Dmaj7  
Lonely as I am, together we cry.

## *REPEAT CHORUS*

## INTERLUDE 2

G*  Gm    F6    E♭maj7  
    Yeah,  yeah,  yeah.

G*  Gm     F6    E♭maj7  
Oh,  no, no, no, yeah, yeah.

G*  Gm     F6    E♭maj7    E♭5          D5   F6  
Love me, I said, yeah, yeah.        One time.

## BRIDGE

G*    Gm  F6   E♭maj7
Under the bridge downtown  is where I drew some blood.
G*    Gm  F6   E♭maj7
Under the bridge downtown  I could not get enough.
G*    Gm  F6   E♭maj7
Under the bridge downtown  forgot about my love.
G*    Gm  F6   E♭maj7
Under the bridge downtown  I gave my life away.
G* Gm F6 E♭maj7
 Yeah, yeah, yeah.

 G* Gm    F6 E♭maj7
 Oh, no, no, no, no, yeah, yeah.
(Away.
 G* Gm    F6 E♭maj7
 Oh, no, I said oh , yeah, yeah.
Away.
 G* Gm    F6 E♭maj7
    Here I stay.
Away.)

## OUTRO

‖: G*  Gm   | F6  E♭maj7 | G*  Gm   | F6  E♭maj7 :‖ G        ‖

# Wonderwall

## Words and Music by Noel Gallagher

(Capo 2nd Fret)

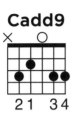
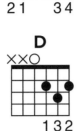
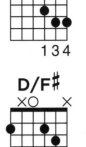
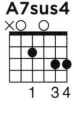
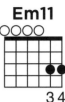

| Em7 | G | Dsus4 | A7sus4 |
| Cadd9 | D | D/F# | Em11 |

## INTRO

**Moderately**

*Play 4 times*

‖: **Em7**　　　　　　**G**　　　｜**Dsus4**　　**A7sus4**　　：‖

## VERSE 1

**Em7**　　　　　**G**　　　　　　　**Dsus4**　　　**A7sus4**
Today, is gonna be the day that they're gonna throw it back to you

**Em7**　　　　　　**G**　　　　　　　**Dsus4**　　　**A7sus4**
By now you should have somehow realized what you gotta do.

**Em7**　　　　　**G**　　**Dsus4**　　**A7sus4**
I don't believe that anybody feels the way I do about you now.

｜**Cadd9**　　　　**Dsus4**　　　　｜**A7sus4**　　　　　　　　‖

## VERSE 2

**Em7**　　　　　　　**G**　　　　　**Dsus4**　　**A7sus4**
Backbeat, the word is on the street that the fire in your heart is out.

**Em7**　　　　　　　**G**　　　　　**Dsus4**　　**A7sus4**
I'm sure you've heard it all before, but you never really had a doubt.

**Em7**　　　　　**G**　　**Dsus4**　　**A7sus4**
I don't believe that anybody feels the way I do about you now.

｜**Em7**　　　　　　**G**　　　　｜**Dsus4**　　**A7sus4**

## PRE-CHORUS 1

Cadd9    D    Em7
And all the roads we have to walk are winding,

Cadd9    D    Em7
and all the lights that lead us there are blinding.

Cadd9    D    G  D/F#  Em7  G    A7sus4
There are many things that I would like to say to you, but I don't know how.

## CHORUS 1

Cadd9  Em7  G    Em7
Because maybe    you're gonna be the one that

Cadd9  Em7  G    Em7
saves me.    And after all

Cadd9  Em7  G    Em7
    you're my wonderwall.

| Cadd9   Em7 | G   Em7 | | Em11 |

## VERSE 3

Em7    G    Dsus4    A7sus4
Today was gonna be the day, but they'll never throw it back to you.

Em7    G    Dsus4    A7sus4
By now you should have somehow realized what you're not to do.

Em7    G  Dsus4    A7sus4
I don't believe that anybody feels the way I do about you now.

| Em7     G | Dsus4   A7sus4 |

## PRE-CHORUS 2

Cadd9    D    Em7
And all the roads that lead you there were winding,

Cadd9    D    Em7
and all the lights that light the way are blinding.

Cadd9    D    G  D/F#  Em7  G    A7sus4
There are many things that I would like to say to you, but I don't know how.

## CHORUS 2

Cadd9    Em7    G         Em7
I said maybe            you're gonna be the one that

Cadd9    Em7   G     Em7
saves me.            And after all

Cadd9   Em7   G         Em7
             you're my wonderwall.

Cadd9   Em7   G   Em7

Cadd9         Em7    G        Em7
I said maybe (I said maybe)    you're gonna be the one that

Cadd9   Em7   G     Em7
saves me.            And after all

Cadd9   Em7   G         Em7
             you're my wonderwall.

Cadd9   Em7   G   Em7

Cadd9         Em7    G        Em7
I said maybe            you're gonna be the one that
          (I said maybe.

Cadd9      Em7     G     Em7
saves me.           You're gonna be the one that
      That saves me.

Cadd9      Em7     G     Em7
saves me.           You're gonna be the one that
      That saves me.

Cadd9      Em7     G  Em7
saves me.
      That saves me.)

## OUTRO

||: Cadd9         Em7     |1., 2., 3.              |4.
                            | G         Em7   :|| G        Em7    ||

# Use Somebody

**Words and Music by Caleb Followill, Nathan Followill, Jared Followill and Matthew Followill**

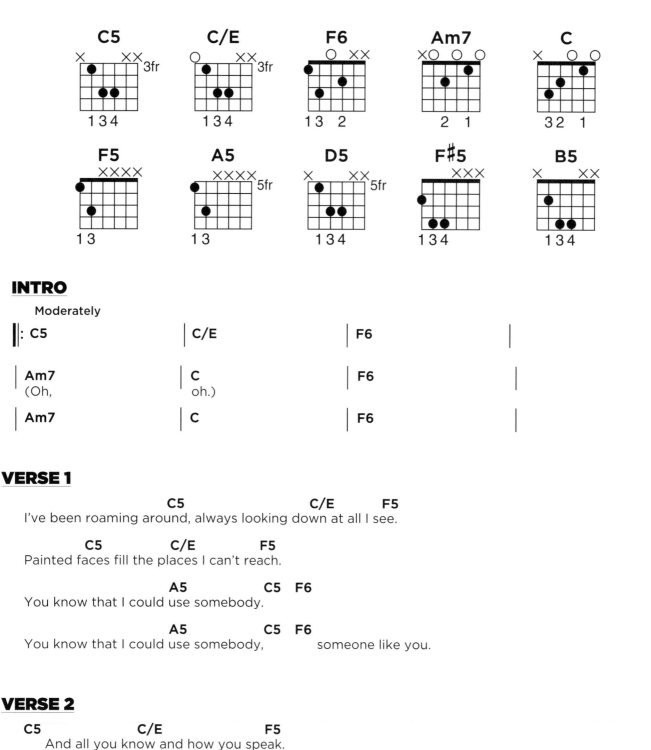

## INTRO

Moderately

```
‖: C5            | C/E           | F6            |             :‖

   Am7           | C             | F6            |             |
   (Oh,            oh.)

   Am7           | C             | F6            |             |
```

## VERSE 1

```
                C5                  C/E        F5
   I've been roaming around, always looking down at all I see.

        C5       C/E       F5
   Painted faces fill the places I can't reach.

                  A5            C5  F6
   You know that I could use somebody.

                  A5            C5  F6
   You know that I could use somebody,        someone like you.
```

## VERSE 2

```
   C5               C/E          F5
      And all you know and how you speak.

        C5         C/E       F5
   Coutless lovers under cover of the street.

                  A5            C5  F6
   You know that I could use somebody.

                  A5            C5  F6
   You know that I could use somebody,        someone like you.
```

## CHORUS 1

‖: **C5** | **C/E** | **F6** | | :‖
(Oh,         oh.

| **Am7** | **C** | **F6** | |
Oh,         oh.

| **Am7** | **C** | **F6** | |
Oh,         oh.)

## VERSE 3

         **C5**                   **C/E**     **F5**
Off in the night while you live it up       I'm off to sleep.

         **C5**          **C/E**      **F5**
waging wars to shake the poet and the beat.

           **A5**         **C5**  **F6**
I hope it's gonna make you notice.

           **A5**         **C5**  **F6**
I hope it's gonna make you notice     someone like me.

## CHORUS 2

‖: **C5** | **C/E** | **F6** | | :‖
(Oh,         oh.)                                          Someone like me.

| **Am7** | **C** | **F6** | |
      Somebody.
(Oh,         oh.)

| **Am7** | **C** | **F6** | | ‖
(Oh,         oh.)

## BRIDGE

  **D5**               **F♯5**
(Oh, let it out. Oh, let it out. Oh, let it out.

    **D5**                    **F♯5**     **B5**  **N.C.**
Oh, let it out. Oh, let it out. Oh, let it out. Oh, let   it out.)

## INTERLUDE

| **C5** | **C/E** | **F6** | | |

| **Am7** | **C** | **F6** | | ‖
                                                   Someone like you,

## CHORUS 3

                                         1., 2.             3.

‖: **Am7** | **C** | **F6** | | :‖
   somebody.                                             Someone like you,

## OUTRO

              **C5**                **C/E**     **F5**
I've been roaming around, always looking down at all I see.

# When I Come Around

Words by Billie Joe
Music by Green Day

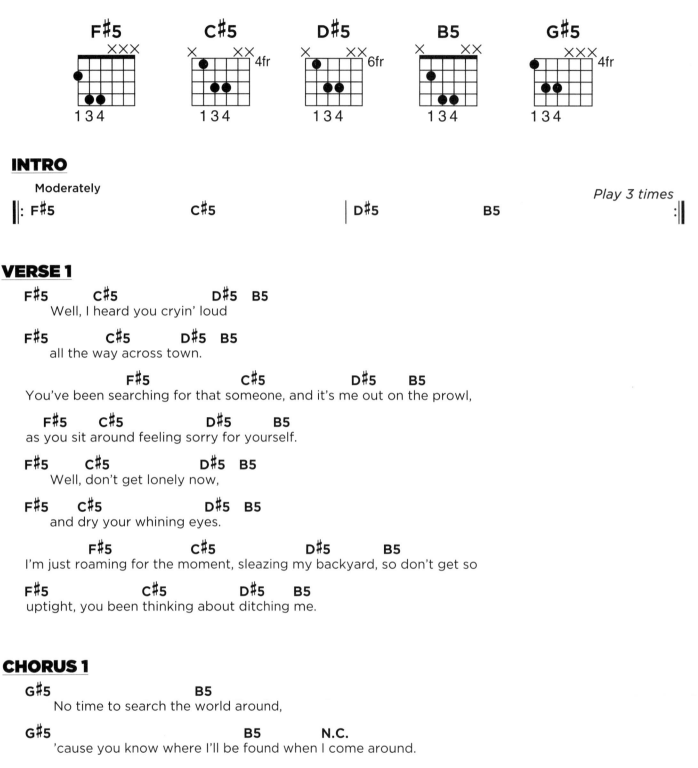

**INTRO**

Moderately

Play 3 times

‖: F♯5          C♯5          | D♯5          B5          :‖

**VERSE 1**

F♯5      C♯5          D♯5   B5
Well, I heard you cryin' loud

F♯5          C♯5          D♯5   B5
all the way across town.

F♯5              C♯5              D♯5      B5
You've been searching for that someone, and it's me out on the prowl,

F♯5    C♯5          D♯5          B5
as you sit around feeling sorry for yourself.

F♯5    C♯5          D♯5   B5
Well, don't get lonely now,

F♯5    C♯5          D♯5   B5
and dry your whining eyes.

F♯5          C♯5              D♯5          B5
I'm just roaming for the moment, sleazing my backyard, so don't get so

F♯5          C♯5      D♯5   B5
uptight, you been thinking about ditching me.

**CHORUS 1**

G♯5                          B5
No time to search the world around,

G♯5                          B5          N.C.
'cause you know where I'll be found when I come around.

| F♯5      C♯5 | D♯5      B5 | F♯5      C♯5 | D♯5      B5 ‖

## VERSE 2

F#5       C#5           D#5  B5
Well, I heard it all before,

F#5   C#5                    D#5  B5
so don't knock down my door.

         F#5       C#5      D#5       B5
I'm a loser and a user so I don't need no accuser to

F#5          C#5         D#5       B5
try and slag me down because I know you're right.

F#5  C#5             D#5  B5
So go do what you like.

F#5   C#5          D#5  B5
Make sure you do it wise.

        F#5         C#5          D#5     B5
You may find out that your self-doubt means nothing was ever there.

       F#5         C#5        D#5  B5
You can't go forcing something if it's just not right.


## *REPEAT CHORUS 1*


## GUITAR SOLO

| F#5       C#5 | D#5     B5 | F#5      C#5 | D#5     B5 ||


## CHORUS 2

G#5                        B5
No time to search the world around,

G#5                          B5       N.C.
'cause you know where I'll be found when I come around.

F#5  C#5  D#5  B5
Oh, when I come around.

F#5  C#5  D#5  B5
Oh, when I come around.

F#5  C#5  D#5  B5
When I come around.

| F#5       C#5 | D#5     B5 ||

# Get Better at Guitar

## ...with these Great Guitar Instruction Books from Hal Leonard!

### 101 GUITAR TIPS
**STUFF ALL THE PROS KNOW AND USE**
*by Adam St. James*
INCLUDES TAB

This book contains invaluable guidance on everything from scales and music theory to truss rod adjustments, proper recording studio set-ups, and much more.

00695737 Book/Online Audio .................................$17.99

### AMAZING PHRASING
*by Tom Kolb*
INCLUDES TAB

This book/audio pack explores all the main components necessary for crafting well-balanced rhythmic and melodic phrases. It also explains how these phrases are put together to form cohesive solos. The companion audio contains 89 demo tracks, most with full-band backing.

00695583 Book/Online Audio .................................$22.99

### ARPEGGIOS FOR THE MODERN GUITARIST
*by Tom Kolb*
INCLUDES TAB

Using this no-nonsense book with online audio, guitarists will learn to apply and execute all types of arpeggio forms using a variety of techniques, including alternate picking, sweep picking, tapping, string skipping, and legato.

00695862 Book/Online Audio .................................$22.99

### BLUES YOU CAN USE
*by John Ganapes*

This comprehensive source for learning blues guitar is designed to develop both your lead and rhythm playing. Includes: 21 complete solos • blues chords, progressions and riffs • turnarounds • movable scales and soloing techniques • string bending • utilizing the entire fingerboard • and more.

00142420 Book/Online Media.................................$22.99

### CONNECTING PENTATONIC PATTERNS
*by Tom Kolb*
INCLUDES TAB

If you've been finding yourself trapped in the pentatonic box, this book is for you! This hands-on book with online audio offers examples for guitar players of all levels, from beginner to advanced. Study this book faithfully, and soon you'll be soloing all over the neck with the greatest of ease.

00696445 Book/Online Audio .................................$24.99

### FRETBOARD MASTERY
*by Troy Stetina*
INCLUDES TAB

Untangle the mysterious regions of the guitar fretboard and unlock your potential. This book familiarizes you with all the shapes you need to know by applying them in real musical examples, thereby reinforcing and reaffirming your newfound knowledge.

00695331 Book/Online Audio .................................$22.99

### GUITAR AEROBICS
*by Troy Nelson*
INCLUDES TAB

Here is a daily dose of guitar "vitamins" to keep your chops fine tuned! Musical styles include rock, blues, jazz, metal, country, and funk. Techniques taught include alternate picking, arpeggios, sweep picking, string skipping, legato, string bending, and rhythm guitar.

00695946 Book/Online Audio .................................$24.99

### GUITAR CLUES
**OPERATION PENTATONIC**
*by Greg Koch*
INCLUDES TAB

Whether you're new to improvising or have been doing it for a while, this book/audio pack will provide loads of delicious licks and tricks that you can use right away, from volume swells and chicken pickin' to intervallic and chordal ideas.

00695827 Book/Online Audio .................................$24.99

### PAT METHENY – GUITAR ETUDES
INCLUDES TAB

Over the years, in many master classes and workshops around the world, Pat has demonstrated the kind of daily workout he puts himself through. This book includes a collection of 14 guitar etudes he created to help you limber up, improve picking technique and build finger independence.

00696587.................................................................$19.99

### PICTURE CHORD ENCYCLOPEDIA

This comprehensive guitar chord resource for all playing styles and levels features five voicings of 44 chord qualities for all twelve keys – 2,640 chords in all! For each, there is a clearly illustrated chord frame, as well as *an actual photo* of the chord being played!.

00695224.................................................................$22.99

### RHYTHM GUITAR 365
*by Troy Nelson*
INCLUDES TAB

This book provides 365 exercises – one for every day of the year! – to keep your rhythm chops fine tuned. Topics covered include: chord theory; the fundamentals of rhythm; fingerpicking; strum patterns; diatonic and non-diatonic progressions; triads; major and minor keys; and more.

00103627 Book/Online Audio .................................$27.99

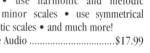

### SCALE CHORD RELATIONSHIPS
*by Michael Mueller & Jeff Schroedl*
INCLUDES TAB

This book/audio pack explains how to: recognize keys • analyze chord progressions • use the modes • play over nondiatonic harmony • use harmonic and melodic minor scales • use symmetrical scales • incorporate exotic scales • and much more!

00695563 Book/Online Audio .................................$17.99

### SPEED MECHANICS FOR LEAD GUITAR
*by Troy Stetina*
INCLUDES TAB

Take your playing to the stratosphere with this advanced lead book which will help you develop speed and precision in today's explosive playing styles. Learn the fastest ways to achieve speed and control, secrets to make your practice time really count, and how to open your ears and make your musical ideas more solid and tangible.

00699323 Book/Online Audio .................................$22.99

### TOTAL ROCK GUITAR
*by Troy Stetina*
INCLUDES TAB

This comprehensive source for learning rock guitar is designed to develop both lead and rhythm playing. It covers: getting a tone that rocks • open chords, power chords and barre chords • riffs, scales and licks • string bending, strumming, and harmonics • and more.

00695246 Book/Online Audio .................................$22.99

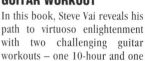

*Guitar World Presents*
### STEVE VAI'S GUITAR WORKOUT
INCLUDES TAB

In this book, Steve Vai reveals his path to virtuoso enlightenment with two challenging guitar workouts – one 10-hour and one 30-hour – which include scale and chord exercises, ear training, sight-reading, music theory, and much more.

00119643.................................................................$16.99

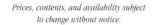

# REALLY EASY GUITAR

Easy-to-follow charts to get you playing right away are presented in these collections of arrangements in chords, lyrics and basic tab for all guitarists.

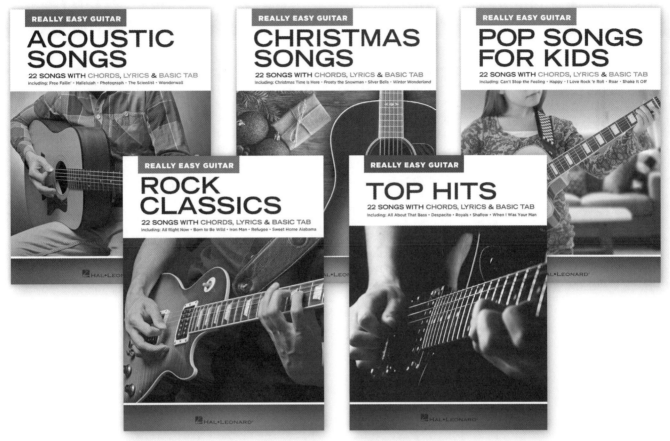

## ACOUSTIC CLASSICS
22 songs: Angie • Best of My Love • Dust in the Wind • Fire and Rain • A Horse with No Name • Layla • More Than a Feeling • Night Moves • Patience • Time in a Bottle • Wanted Dead or Alive • and more.
00300600 ............................................................................ $9.99

## ACOUSTIC SONGS
22 songs: Free Fallin' • Good Riddance (Time of Your Life) • Hallelujah • I'm Yours • Losing My Religion • Mr. Jones • Photograph • Riptide • The Scientist • Wonderwall • and more.
00286663 ..........................................................................$10.99

## ADELE
22 songs: All I Ask • Chasing Pavements • Daydreamer • Easy On Me • Hello • I Drink Wine • Love in the Dark • Lovesong • Make You Feel My Love • Turning Tables • Water Under the Bridge • and more.
00399557 ..........................................................................$12.99

## THE BEATLES FOR KIDS
14 songs: All You Need Is Love • Blackbird • Good Day Sunshine • Here Comes the Sun • I Want to Hold Your Hand • Let It Be • With a Little Help from My Friends • Yellow Submarine • and more.
00346031 ..........................................................................$12.99

## CHRISTMAS CLASSICS
22 Christmas carols: Away in a Manger • Deck the Hall • It Came upon the Midnight Clear • Jingle Bells • Silent Night • The Twelve Days of Christmas • We Wish You a Merry Christmas • and more.
00348327 ..........................................................................$10.99

## CHRISTMAS SONGS
22 holiday favorites: Blue Christmas • Christmas Time Is Here • Frosty the Snowman • Have Yourself a Merry Little Christmas • Mary, Did You Know? • Silver Bells • Winter Wonderland • and more.
00294775 ............................................................................ $9.99

## THE DOORS
22 songs: Break on Through to the Other Side • Hello, I Love You (Won't You Tell Me Your Name?) • L.A. Woman • Light My Fire • Love Her Madly • People Are Strange • Riders on the Storm • Touch Me • and more.
00345890 ............................................................................ $9.99

## BILLIE EILISH
14 songs: All the Good Girls Go to Hell • Bad Guy • Everything I Wanted • Idontwannabeyouanymore • No Time to Die • Ocean Eyes • Six Feet Under • Wish You Were Gay • and more.
00346351 ..........................................................................$12.99

## POP SONGS FOR KIDS
22 songs: Brave • Can't Stop the Feeling • Happy • I Love Rock 'N Roll • Let It Go • Roar • Shake It Off • We Got the Beat • and more.
00286698 ..........................................................................$10.99

## ROCK CLASSICS
22 songs: All Right Now • Born to Be Wild • Don't Fear the Reaper • Hey Joe • Iron Man • Old Time Rock & Roll • Refugee • Sweet Home Alabama • You Shook Me All Night Long • and more.
00286699 ..........................................................................$10.99

## TAYLOR SWIFT
22 hits: Back to December • Cardigan • Exile • Look What You Made Me Do • Mean • The One • Our Song • Safe & Sound • Teardrops on My Guitar • We Are Never Ever Getting Back Together • White Horse • You Need to Calm Down • and more.
00356881..........................................................................$12.99

## TOP HITS
22 hits: All About That Bass • All of Me • Despacito • Love Yourself • Royals • Say Something • Shallow • Someone like You • This Is Me • A Thousand Years • When I Was Your Man • and more.
00300599 ..........................................................................$10.99

**HAL•LEONARD®**
halleonard.com
Prices, contents and availability subject to change without notice. All prices listed in U.S. funds.

# EASY GUITAR WITH NOTES & TAB

*This series features simplified arrangements with notes, tab, chord charts, and strum and pick patterns.*

## MIXED FOLIOS

| | | |
|---|---|---|
| 00702287 | Acoustic | $19.99 |
| 00702002 | Acoustic Rock Hits for Easy Guitar | $17.99 |
| 00702166 | All-Time Best Guitar Collection | $29.99 |
| 00702232 | Best Acoustic Songs for Easy Guitar | $16.99 |
| 00119835 | Best Children's Songs | $16.99 |
| 00703055 | The Big Book of Nursery Rhymes & Children's Songs | $16.99 |
| 00698978 | Big Christmas Collection | $19.99 |
| 00702394 | Bluegrass Songs for Easy Guitar | $15.99 |
| 00289632 | Bohemian Rhapsody | $19.99 |
| 00703387 | Celtic Classics | $16.99 |
| 00224808 | Chart Hits of 2016-2017 | $14.99 |
| 00267383 | Chart Hits of 2017-2018 | $14.99 |
| 00334293 | Chart Hits of 2019-2020 | $16.99 |
| 00403479 | Chart Hits of 2021-2022 | $16.99 |
| 00702149 | Children's Christian Songbook | $9.99 |
| 00702028 | Christmas Classics | $9.99 |
| 00101779 | Christmas Guitar | $16.99 |
| 00702141 | Classic Rock | $8.95 |
| 00159642 | Classical Melodies | $12.99 |
| 00253933 | Disney/Pixar's Coco | $19.99 |
| 00702203 | CMT's 100 Greatest Country Songs | $34.99 |
| 00702283 | The Contemporary Christian Collection | $16.99 |

| | | |
|---|---|---|
| 00196954 | Contemporary Disney | $19.99 |
| 00702239 | Country Classics for Easy Guitar | $24.99 |
| 00702257 | Easy Acoustic Guitar Songs | $17.99 |
| 00702041 | Favorite Hymns for Easy Guitar | $12.99 |
| 00222701 | Folk Pop Songs | $19.99 |
| 00126894 | Frozen | $14.99 |
| 00333922 | Frozen 2 | $14.99 |
| 00702286 | Glee | $16.99 |
| 00702160 | The Great American Country Songbook | $19.99 |
| 00702148 | Great American Gospel for Guitar | $14.99 |
| 00702050 | Great Classical Themes for Easy Guitar | $9.99 |
| 00148030 | Halloween Guitar Songs | $17.99 |
| 00702273 | Irish Songs | $14.99 |
| 00192503 | Jazz Classics for Easy Guitar | $16.99 |
| 00702275 | Jazz Favorites for Easy Guitar | $17.99 |
| 00702274 | Jazz Standards for Easy Guitar | $19.99 |
| 00702162 | Jumbo Easy Guitar Songbook | $24.99 |
| 00232285 | La La Land | $16.99 |
| 00702258 | Legends of Rock | $14.99 |
| 00702189 | MTV's 100 Greatest Pop Songs | $34.99 |
| 00702272 | 1950s Rock | $16.99 |
| 00702271 | 1960s Rock | $16.99 |
| 00702270 | 1970s Rock | $24.99 |
| 00702269 | 1980s Rock | $16.99 |

| | | |
|---|---|---|
| 00702268 | 1990s Rock | $24.99 |
| 00369043 | Rock Songs for Kids | $14.99 |
| 00109725 | Once | $14.99 |
| 00702187 | Selections from O Brother Where Art Thou? | $19.99 |
| 00702178 | 100 Songs for Kids | $16.99 |
| 00702515 | Pirates of the Caribbean | $17.99 |
| 00702125 | Praise and Worship for Guitar | $14.99 |
| 00287930 | Songs from *A Star Is Born, The Greatest Showman, La La Land,* and More Movie Musicals | $16.99 |
| 00702285 | Southern Rock Hits | $12.99 |
| 00156420 | Star Wars Music | $16.99 |
| 00121535 | 30 Easy Celtic Guitar Solos | $16.99 |
| 00244654 | Top Hits of 2017 | $14.99 |
| 00283786 | Top Hits of 2018 | $14.99 |
| 00302269 | Top Hits of 2019 | $14.99 |
| 00355779 | Top Hits of 2020 | $14.99 |
| 00374083 | Top Hits of 2021 | $16.99 |
| 00702294 | Top Worship Hits | $17.99 |
| 00702255 | VH1's 100 Greatest Hard Rock Songs | $39.99 |
| 00702175 | VH1's 100 Greatest Songs of Rock and Roll | $34.99 |
| 00702253 | Wicked | $12.99 |

## ARTIST COLLECTIONS

| | | |
|---|---|---|
| 00702267 | AC/DC for Easy Guitar | $17.99 |
| 00156221 | Adele – 25 | $16.99 |
| 00396889 | Adele – 30 | $19.99 |
| 00702040 | Best of the Allman Brothers | $16.99 |
| 00702865 | J.S. Bach for Easy Guitar | $15.99 |
| 00702169 | Best of The Beach Boys | $16.99 |
| 00702292 | The Beatles — 1 | $22.99 |
| 00125796 | Best of Chuck Berry | $16.99 |
| 00702201 | The Essential Black Sabbath | $15.99 |
| 00702250 | blink-182 — Greatest Hits | $19.99 |
| 02501615 | Zac Brown Band — The Foundation | $19.99 |
| 02501621 | Zac Brown Band — You Get What You Give | $16.99 |
| 00702043 | Best of Johnny Cash | $19.99 |
| 00702090 | Eric Clapton's Best | $16.99 |
| 00702086 | Eric Clapton — from the Album Unplugged | $17.99 |
| 00702202 | The Essential Eric Clapton | $19.99 |
| 00702053 | Best of Patsy Cline | $17.99 |
| 00222697 | Very Best of Coldplay – 2nd Edition | $17.99 |
| 00702229 | The Very Best of Creedence Clearwater Revival | $16.99 |
| 00702145 | Best of Jim Croce | $16.99 |
| 00702278 | Crosby, Stills & Nash | $12.99 |
| 14042809 | Bob Dylan | $15.99 |
| 00702276 | Fleetwood Mac — Easy Guitar Collection | $17.99 |
| 00139462 | The Very Best of Grateful Dead | $17.99 |
| 00702136 | Best of Merle Haggard | $19.99 |
| 00702227 | Jimi Hendrix — Smash Hits | $19.99 |
| 00702288 | Best of Hillsong United | $12.99 |
| 00702236 | Best of Antonio Carlos Jobim | $15.99 |

| | | |
|---|---|---|
| 00702245 | Elton John — Greatest Hits 1970–2002 | $19.99 |
| 00129855 | Jack Johnson | $17.99 |
| 00702204 | Robert Johnson | $16.99 |
| 00702234 | Selections from Toby Keith — 35 Biggest Hits | $12.95 |
| 00702003 | Kiss | $16.99 |
| 00702216 | Lynyrd Skynyrd | $17.99 |
| 00702182 | The Essential Bob Marley | $17.99 |
| 00146081 | Maroon 5 | $14.99 |
| 00121925 | Bruno Mars – Unorthodox Jukebox | $12.99 |
| 00702248 | Paul McCartney — All the Best | $14.99 |
| 00125484 | The Best of MercyMe | $12.99 |
| 00702209 | Steve Miller Band — Young Hearts (Greatest Hits) | $12.95 |
| 00124167 | Jason Mraz | $15.99 |
| 00702096 | Best of Nirvana | $17.99 |
| 00702211 | The Offspring — Greatest Hits | $17.99 |
| 00138026 | One Direction | $17.99 |
| 00702030 | Best of Roy Orbison | $17.99 |
| 00702144 | Best of Ozzy Osbourne | $14.99 |
| 00702279 | Tom Petty | $17.99 |
| 00102911 | Pink Floyd | $17.99 |
| 00702139 | Elvis Country Favorites | $19.99 |
| 00702293 | The Very Best of Prince | $22.99 |
| 00699415 | Best of Queen for Guitar | $16.99 |
| 00109279 | Best of R.E.M. | $14.99 |
| 00702208 | Red Hot Chili Peppers — Greatest Hits | $19.99 |
| 00198960 | The Rolling Stones | $17.99 |
| 00174793 | The Very Best of Santana | $16.99 |
| 00702196 | Best of Bob Seger | $16.99 |
| 00146046 | Ed Sheeran | $19.99 |

| | | |
|---|---|---|
| 00702252 | Frank Sinatra — Nothing But the Best | $12.99 |
| 00702010 | Best of Rod Stewart | $17.99 |
| 00702049 | Best of George Strait | $17.99 |
| 00702259 | Taylor Swift for Easy Guitar | $15.99 |
| 00359800 | Taylor Swift – Easy Guitar Anthology | $24.99 |
| 00702260 | Taylor Swift — Fearless | $14.99 |
| 00139727 | Taylor Swift — 1989 | $19.99 |
| 00115960 | Taylor Swift — Red | $16.99 |
| 00253667 | Taylor Swift — Reputation | $17.99 |
| 00702290 | Taylor Swift — Speak Now | $16.99 |
| 00232849 | Chris Tomlin Collection – 2nd Edition | $14.99 |
| 00702226 | Chris Tomlin — See the Morning | $12.95 |
| 00148643 | Train | $14.99 |
| 00702427 | U2 — 18 Singles | $19.99 |
| 00702108 | Best of Stevie Ray Vaughan | $17.99 |
| 00279005 | The Who | $14.99 |
| 00702123 | Best of Hank Williams | $15.99 |
| 00194548 | Best of John Williams | $14.99 |
| 00702228 | Neil Young — Greatest Hits | $17.99 |
| 00119133 | Neil Young — Harvest | $16.99 |

Prices, contents and availability subject to change without notice.

HAL•LEONARD®

Visit Hal Leonard online at halleonard.com